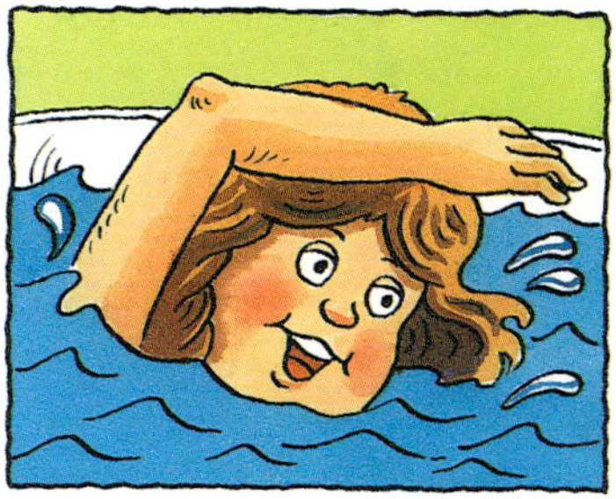

Sometimes

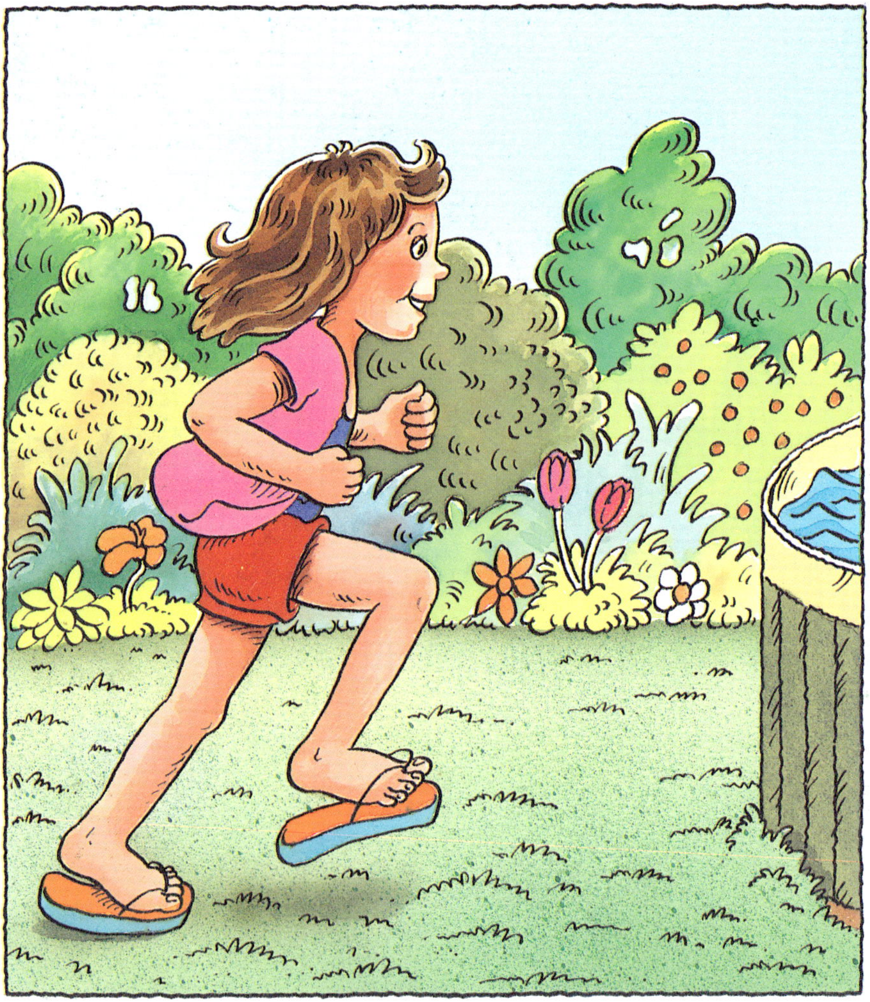

Sometimes I run.

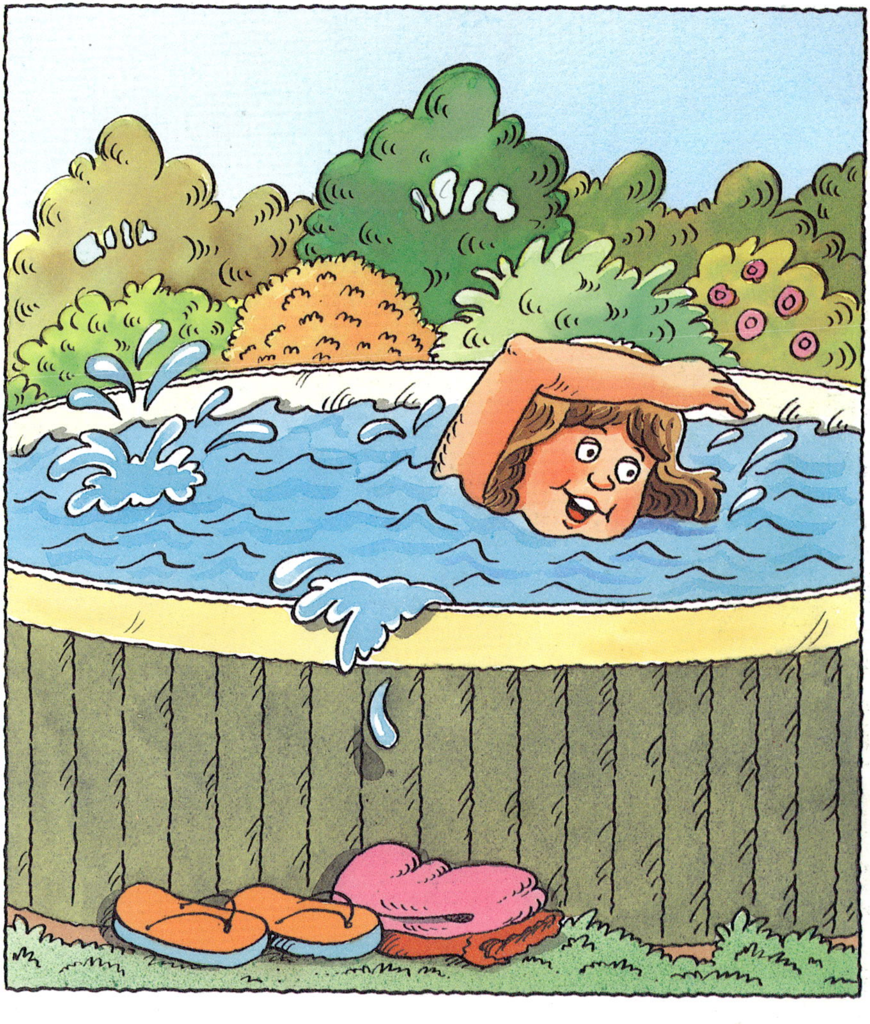

Sometimes I swim.

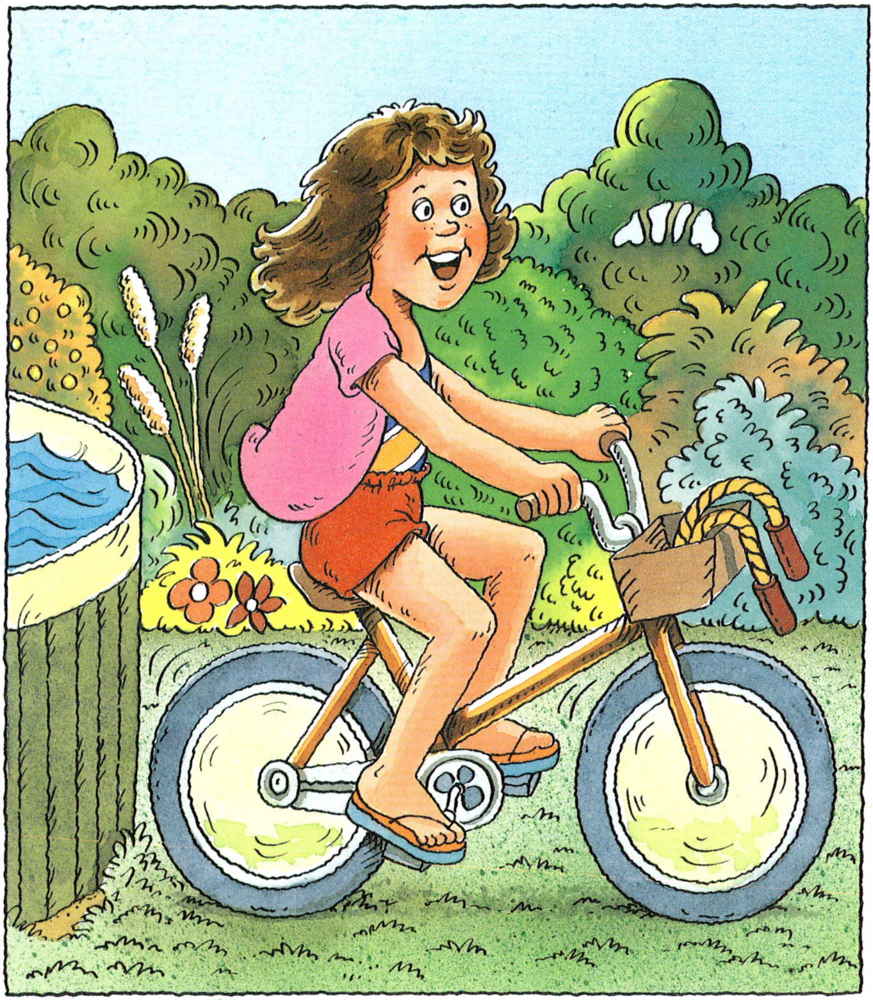

Sometimes I ride.

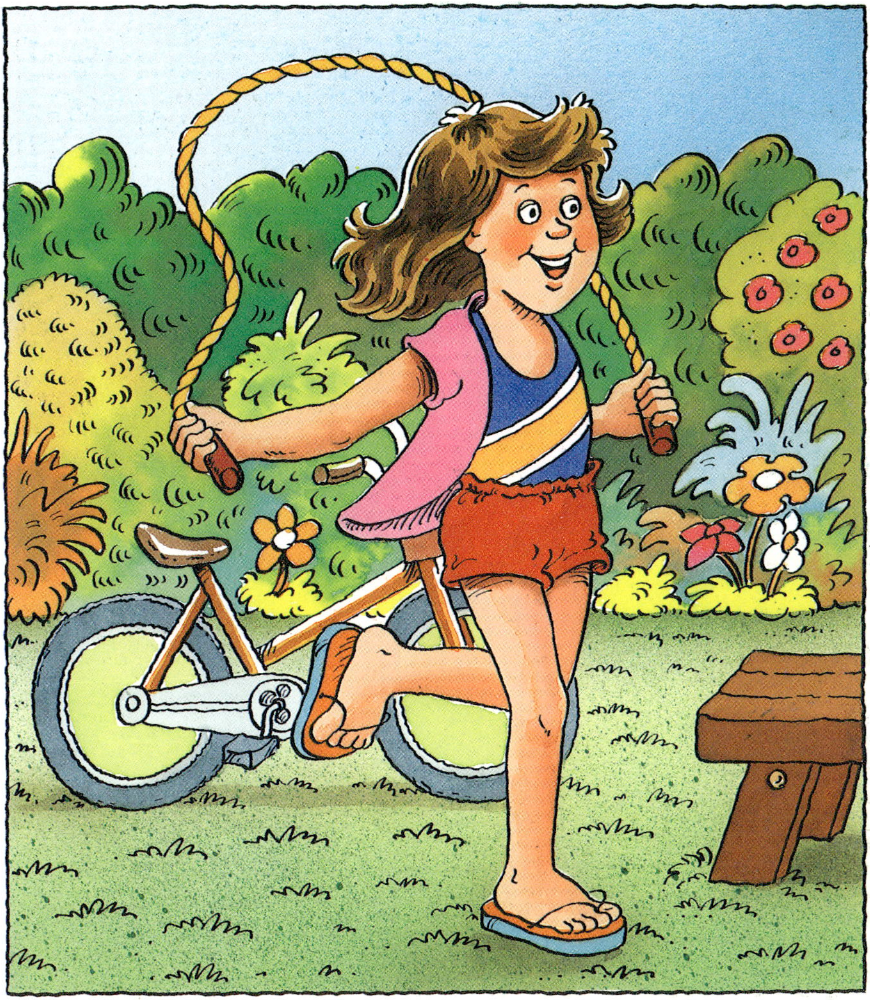

Sometimes I jump.

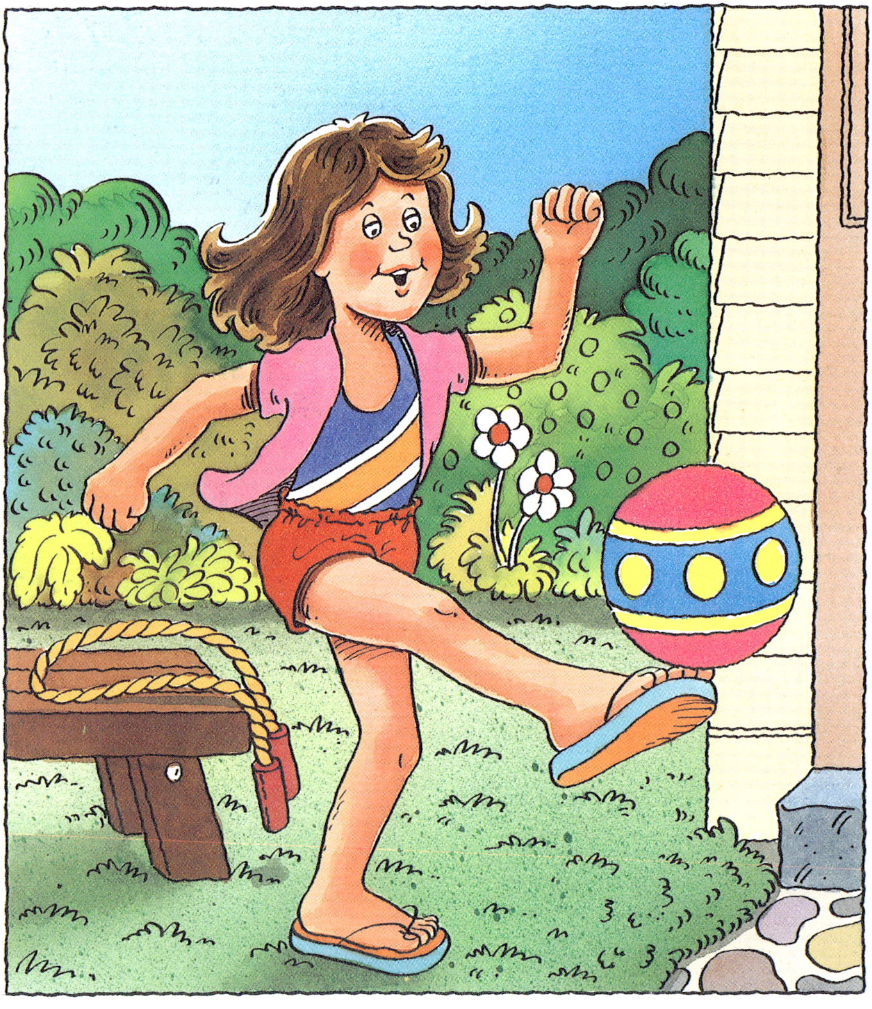

Sometimes I kick.

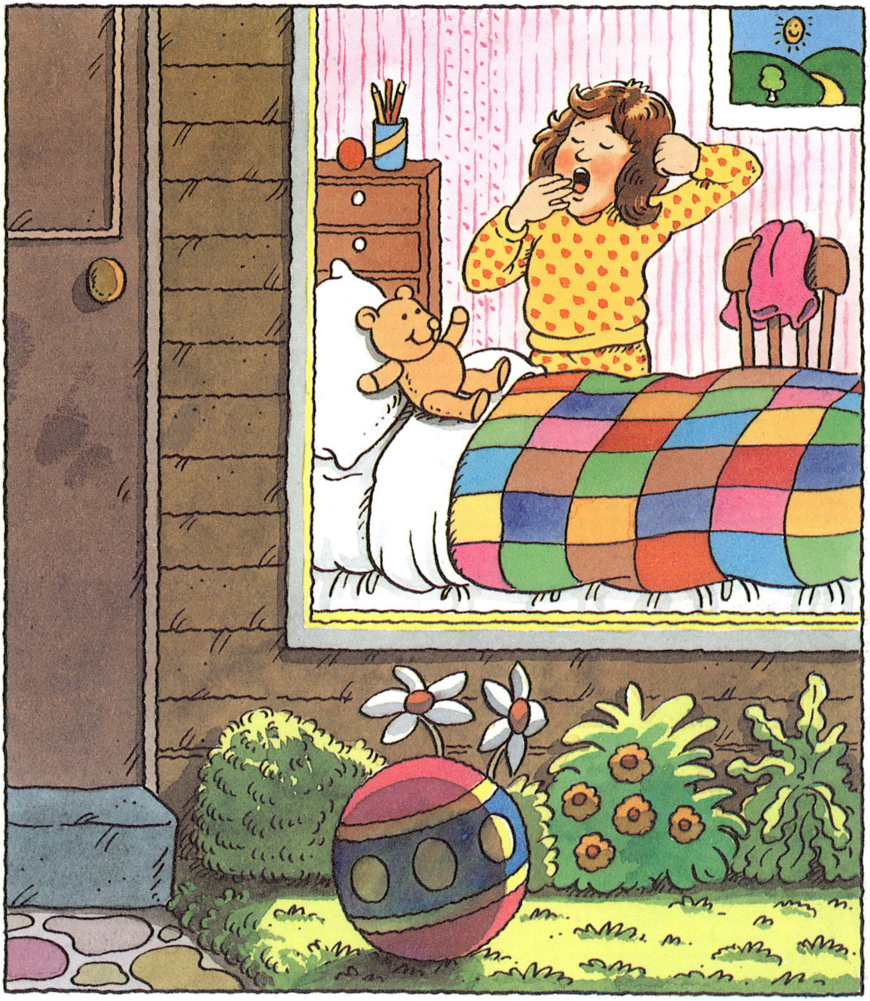

Sometimes I...

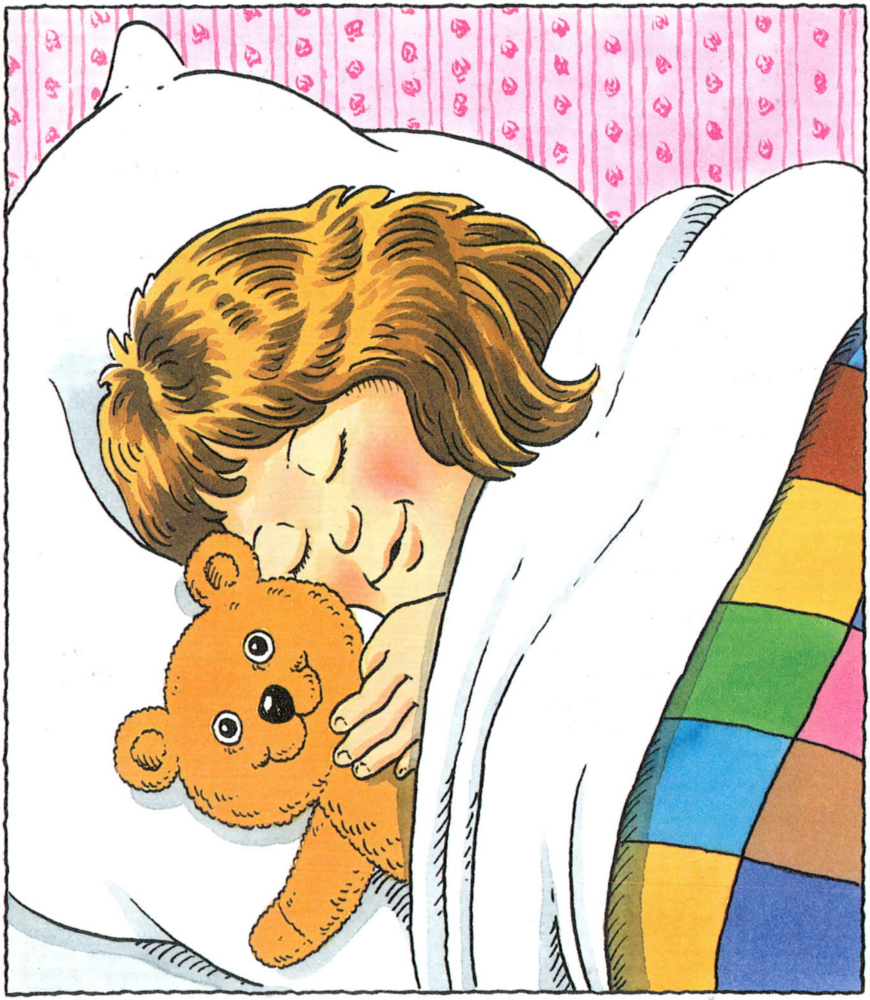

sleep.